IMAGES
of America

The Royal Air Force Over Florida

IMAGES
of America

The Royal Air Force Over Florida

A.M. de Quesada

ISBN 978-1-5316-4533-5

Published by Arcadia Publishing
Charleston, South Carolina

Library of Congress Catalog Card Number: 98-87572

For all general information contact Arcadia Publishing at:
Telephone 843-853-2070
Fax 843-853-0044
E-mail sales@arcadiapublishing.com
For customer service and orders:
Toll-Free 1-888-313-2665

Visit us on the Internet at www.arcadiapublishing.com

This work is dedicated to the memory of the 23 RAF cadets buried in Arcadia with their instructor, John Paul Riddle.

Contents

ACKNOWLEDGMENTS

I would like to thank the following individuals and institutions that made this book possible: Peter Brannan, former BFTS #5 Cadet (Course 25); Hugh Williams, former BFTS #5 Cadet; ADEQ Historical Resources, Inc.; John W. Cook, USAAF, former BFTS #5 Cadet (Course 14); Eric Carlson, former Riddle-McKay Aero College instructor; A.M. de Quesada, M.D.; J.B. McCrary, Director, Clewiston Museum; Vincent Luisi, Director, Dunedin Historical Museum; Paul Eugen Camp, Special Collections, University of South Florida; Special Collections, Lakeland Public Library; John Lindstrom, St. Petersburg Historical Museum; The Florida Historical Aviation Society; David Parry, Photograph Archive, Imperial War Museum; Fred Aldworth, Air Force Association of Canada; 5 BFTS Association; The Royal Air Force; the United States Air Force; and National Archives.

Introduction

To this day, a bit of Britain can be found in a small Florida town. Twenty-three Royal Air Force Cadets sleep eternally in a shaded and peaceful cemetery in Arcadia. They came across the Atlantic to learn how to fly; however, for them the war would soon clip their wings forever. This is their story.

Poland, Norway, Denmark, Belgium, Holland—they all succumbed. Then France. Hitler's schedule for destruction took a definite stand when France was overwhelmingly defeated, June 22, 1940. Churchill's defiant refusal of Hitler's offer for British capitulation led to the Nazi's final preparation for the invasion of Britain. First came the preliminary stage of the Battle of Britain, the world's first all-air battle. The Nazi Luftwaffe, headed by Hermann Göring, began to bomb shipping and the fringes of the British Isles by July 10, 1940. On August 8 the all-out air-blitz of England itself began. Britain, standing alone, was faced with almost certain death.

Operational airdromes for the defense of Britain crowded the British Isles. Flying training schools required space needed for the defense and enemy bombing interrupted training. Royal Air Force (RAF) training airfields were bombed for the first time on August 13. But it wasn't until eight months later, on April 13, 1941, that it was agreed at a conference between RAF Chief of Training Air Vice-Marshall Garrod and Commanding General of the U.S. Air Service General H.H. Arnold that a part of the training facilities in the United States would be turned over to the British. Arrangements for the establishment of six British flying training schools in the United States had already been made.

The establishment of British and American flying training schools in the United States finally took shape and southern Florida received its share in the months before the Japanese attack upon Pearl Harbor. The city of Arcadia in south-central Florida became a pivotal point for two important British training schools: the British No. 5 at Riddle Field, Clewiston, and the U.S. School at Carlstrom and Dorr Fields, Arcadia. Carlstrom Field, a World War I army airfield, reopened in June 1941; Riddle Field, headed by John Paul Riddle, opened for training in September.

At the time of the first death of a RAF cadet at either of the two schools, July 22, 1941, by request of the British authorities, arrangements for a burial site in Arcadia's Oak Ridge Cemetery were expeditiously made by Paul P. Speer, Arcadia's city recorder and manager, acting for the city on behalf of the British. A cemetery lot was assigned sufficient for eight burials with adequate areas bordering north and south for expansion. As it turned out, five lots in all were set aside for British burials. Although three accommodated the final 23 burials, the extra two lots provide an appropriate area for meditation and memorials. These lots have not been deeded to the British government as the very nature of their use assures permanency.

At the end of the war, when training was discontinued, there was a marked difference in the number of deaths occurring at the two flying schools noted above. At Arcadia, there were only two deaths, neither of which was due to an aircraft accident. On the other hand, at Clewiston there was a total of 21 deaths, 19 of which were due to aircraft accidents. The reason for this difference was due to the type of aircraft used, together with the training requirements. Carlstrom Field at Arcadia was devoted entirely to primary training and airplanes of simple design were used, such as the Stearman PT-17s. At Clewiston, basic and advanced trainers (BT-13s and AT-6s), as well as primary trainers, were used. The former planes have much greater power with complicated equipment and panels suitable for instrument, blind, and night flying.

Though tragic, the deaths were considered low in view of the number of RAF cadets that attended the various schools scattered throughout central and southern Florida during the war. From 1941 to 1945, the Lodwick School of Aeronautics of Lakeland trained 8,825 cadets, of which 1,327 were British, while the schools in Arcadia and Clewiston have trained well over 1,879 British cadets. Of the six British flying training schools in the United States, BFTS #5 in Clewiston, Florida, received the highest performance rating.

The following RAF cadets are buried in the peaceful Florida cemetery: Charles F. Russell (†July 22, 1941); Louis Wells (†December 9, 1941); Alfred T. Lloyd (†January 4, 1942); Roger B. Crosskey (†January 20, 1942); William Meekin (†June 30, 1942); Richard B. Thorp (†July 16, 1942); Geoffrey R. King (†December 3, 1942); Ronald A. Purrett (†December 12, 1942); Derek R. Clandillion (†January 19, 1943); John A. Clay (†January 19, 1943); Forbes McKenzie Robertson (†April 24, 1943); Marvin H.E. Thomas (†April 28, 1943); Dennis H. Washer (†April 28, 1943); Leonard G. Stone (†August 24, 1943); Edward C.F. Vosper (†August 24, 1943); George H. Wilson (†September 15, 1943); Robert A. Wood (†September 15, 1943); Anthony J. Oakley (†January 14, 1944); Thomas J. Parry (†January 14, 1944); Michael K. Hinds (†July 13, 1944); Lionel M. Viggers (†October 4, 1944); Horace Bowley-Booth (†May 4, 1945); and Thomas W. Calderhead (†May 4, 1945). Decades later an addition was added to the British plot, the former owner of Riddle Field (British Flying Training School No. 5), John Paul Riddle, was laid to rest in 1989 alongside the cadets he had trained during the war.

Each year, on Memorial Day, now the last Monday in May, a formal commemorative service is conducted graveside at the British plot in Arcadia's Oak Ridge Cemetery by the Rotary Club of Arcadia. Many members of the Sarasota Scottish Society, Daughters of the British Empire, Canadian organizations in southern Florida, British veterans and former instructors, as well as townspeople take part in and attend the ceremony which honors these 23 RAF cadets and their instructor who "crossed the river to rest in the shade of the trees." This is not the end, for their story is just about to begin . . .

One

Lodwick School of Aeronautics: Lakeland

The Lakeland Municipal Airport hanger is shown here being moved to its new location with the help of mules. In 1940, the U.S. Army began looking for alternative sites for a primary pilot training school. Lakeland was chosen and as part of an agreement between the army and the City of Lakeland the old Lakeland Municipal Airport hangar was moved to its new location. (Courtesy Lakeland Public Library.)

The Lakeland school was under construction in 1940. (Courtesy Lakeland Public Library.)

This aerial view shows the Lodwick School of Aeronautics complex. Next to the hangars there were five buildings that consisted of two dormitories for 150 cadets, one combination recreation hall/hospital, one combination mess hall/kitchen, and one academic hall for classes. (Courtesy Lakeland Public Library.)

A group of Stearman P-17s waiting to train air cadets at the Lakeland School of Aeronautics in Lakeland. In July 1942 the facility became the Lodwick School of Aeronautics. Established in 1940 with a staff of civilian and military instructors, the school was to help train army officers to fly in the new Army Air Force. (Courtesy Lakeland Public Library.)

These were first Royal Air Force cadets to arrive at the Lakeland school to receive their flight training, 1941. When the RAF arrived changes were made in the training program due to cultural, linguistics, and military customs of the cadets and the RAF. (Courtesy Lakeland Public Library.)

Army air cadets from the Lodwick School of Aeronautics parade through the streets of Lakeland. Note the distinctive flag made for the school. (Courtesy Lakeland Public Library.)

A detachment of RAF cadets march through downtown Lakeland, in a photograph taken between 1941 and 1942. The cadets, both American and British, were often asked to participate in local parades and festivals. Note that the cadets have adopted U.S. khaki dress but still retained their British headgear and insignias. (Courtesy Lakeland Public Library.)

Aviation cadets at most primary pilot training schools were required to be between 18 and 36 years old, and in lieu of at least two years of college he had to pass some academic screening tests as well as some basic tests for good health. The 10-week training program was tough and intense. Many cadets were eliminated before completion. (Courtesy Lakeland Public Library.)

Stearman P-17's were two seaters with a 7-cylinder Continental engine. These aircraft, which became the workhorse in the training of pilots, could be found at army and navy air force training schools and air fields. There were three types of aircraft used by the army for primary training: Boeing (Stearman), the Fairchild, and the Ryan. (Courtesy Lakeland Public Library.)

Ground school provided the academic and technical part of primary training. Cadets were required a specific amount of class time in the following areas: 20 hours in Navigation; 40–60 hours in Aircraft and Engines; 6–9 hours in Aircraft Identification; and approximately 30 hours in Code, Weather, Mathematics, and Chemical Warfare Defense. Most weeks the cadets trained from Monday through Saturday, with a daily routine starting at 6 a.m. Some days they worked until 9 p.m. (Courtesy Lakeland Public Library.)

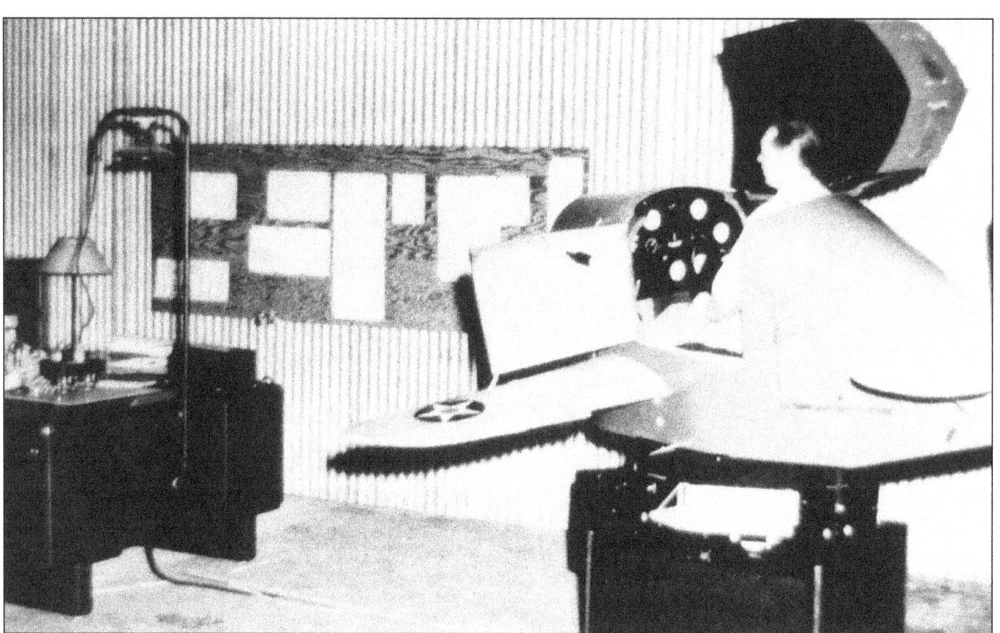

Link trainers simulated flight and cockpit conditions similar to those encountered in a cockpit of a real aircraft. They were affixed with radios so that instructors could be in contact with the cadets at all times. Cadets had to spend a minimum of five hours using the flight simulator. (Courtesy Lakeland Public Library.)

An instructor dressed in a flight suit demonstrates jumping techniques to the cadets in a Lakeland Municipal swimming pool. Cadets were taught how to bail out in cases when they were over water. (Courtesy Lakeland Public Library.)

Cadets are shown here being issued aviation equipment such as a flying suit, leather jacket, goggles, and a Gosport flying helmet. (Courtesy Lakeland Public Library.)

This was one of the ready rooms at the Lodwick School of Aeronautics. Note the table in the back showing the outlines of the runways of the school. (Courtesy Lakeland Public Library.)

Cadets gather around an instructor at a dispatch booth. (Courtesy Lakeland Public Library.)

After fulfilling all requirements, a cadet gets into a plane with his instructor for his first flight. With time, the instructor would gradually give his student more responsibility to the point where he could fly solo. (Courtesy Lakeland Public Library.)

A trainer takes off from the runways of the Lodwick School of Aeronautics. (Courtesy Lakeland Public Library.)

Cadets and instructors return from flight training. (Courtesy Lakeland Public Library.)

With the British RAF cadets came their national pastime—cricket. Here a game is being played between the cadets and the local people of Lakeland on June 5, 1941. (Courtesy Lakeland Public Library.)

As part of the physical training for the cadets, boxing was encouraged as an athletic activity, as demonstrated here by an anxious cadet who wanted to lay his mittens on one of the axis leaders. (Courtesy Lakeland Public Library.)

Cadets also had to master the obstacle course located near their barracks. (Courtesy Lakeland Public Library.)

Military discipline and training was also taught at the school, as evidenced by the cadets standing in formation for a Saturday morning inspection. "Hazing" did occur; however, it was the responsibility of the officers and instructors to control the cadets from getting out of control. (Courtesy Lakeland Public Library.)

Cadets await the order to commence eating their meals at the mess hall. (Courtesy Lakeland Public Library.)

Air cadets walk in front of a hangar at another training field associated with Albert Lodwick, the Lodwick Aviation Military Academy in Avon Park. (Courtesy ADEQ Historical Resources, Inc.)

Albert Lodwick (middle of the three standing over the cockpit) is shown entertaining a committee from Avon Park in Lakeland on July 9, 1941. A contract between Avon Park and Lodwick was signed for a primary pilot school to be opened in Avon Park in October. (Courtesy Lakeland Public Library.)

These cadets, at a morning roll call in 1941, are in front of the former Highland Lakes Hotel. During the war it was converted into a barracks for the Lodwick Aviation Military Academy in Avon Park. After the war the building was turned into a hospital. (Courtesy Lakeland Public Library.)

Throughout the war years, when both schools were operating there were only eight fatalities. Cadets were trained in emergency landing techniques so that one could walk away from a crash like the one pictured here. (Courtesy Lakeland Public Library.)

Flight maintenance was the most important job that a contractor could provide for the army. The mechanics were responsible for the daily maintenance and repair for all aircraft assigned to the schools. These mechanics are removing an engine in order to service it. (Courtesy Lakeland Public Library.)

As part of flight maintenance these workers are applying cellulose nitrate and cellulose butyrate over the fabric-covered wings in order to decrease drag and provide protection from fuel, exhaust residue, and the harmful effects of the sun. (Courtesy Lakeland Public Library.)

The schools provided jobs for hundreds of local residents from Lakeland and Avon Park, as well as their surrounding areas. Pictured here are some of the civilian employees from the Lodwick Aviation Military Academy in Avon Park in 1943. Many of these employees worked as maintenance flight crews and/or as administrative personnel. (Courtesy Lakeland Public Library.)

This is a view of the Highland Lakes Hotel in January 1943. The hotel had been converted into living quarters for air cadets attending the Lodwick Aviation Military Academy in Avon Park. (Courtesy ADEQ Historical Resources, Inc.)

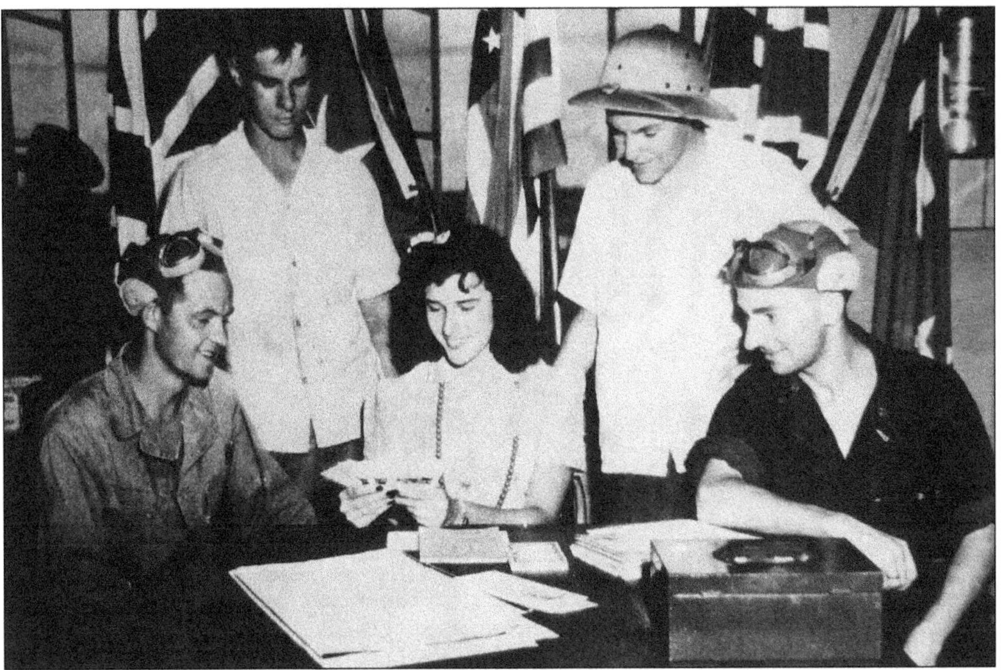

In 1942 a war bond office opened at the school in Avon Park. American and RAF cadets, with their respective flags symbolically behind them, are seen helping a local young girl in a war bond drive. (Courtesy Lakeland Public Library.)

The first graduation of the RAF cadets from the Lakeland school was held at the school on August 16, 1941. The event received wide news coverage from local and national syndicates, as well as from British presses. Handing out diplomas is Florida Governor Spessard Holland, with Albert I. Lodwick, in a white suit, beside him. (Courtesy Lakeland Public Library.)

Spessard Holland is seen here handing out diplomas to the RAF cadets upon their graduation. Holland was noted as saying to the British airmen, "We think of you as eagles going out to fight for the right." (Courtesy Lakeland Public Library.)

Upon their graduation, RAF cadets were able to return to England to fly against the Luftwaffe. Forming a "V" for "Victory," these cadets show off their enthusiasm as airmen. The last RAF class in Lakeland was held in October 1942; after that, the British consolidated their cadets to British Flying Training School No. 5 in Clewiston, Florida. By 1944 the RAF adopted the American training system for aircrew selection and classification, indicating their respect for the American system. From 1940 to 1945, the Lakeland school trained 8,825 cadets, of which 1,327 were British. (Courtesy Lakeland Public Library.)

Two

Riddle Aero. Institute:
Carlstrom and Dorr Fields, Arcadia

This Stearman trainer was photographed in 1941 over Carlstrom Field. The field began its career as a World War I army airfield. Carlstrom and Dorr Fields were twin installations located near Arcadia and were the earliest stations that provided aviation training for the army. Construction began in 1917, and by early 1918, aviation troops were moved in as soon as the perimeter clearing was completed. Hundreds of pilots were trained at these two fields. Several were lost in crashes and there were instances where airplanes and pilots completely disappeared in the Everglades. As late as 1939, the wreckage of a World War I Jennie with the remains of its pilots was found in a remote area. (Courtesy Imperial War Museum.)

The army closed Carlstrom and Dorr Fields in 1924. In June 1941, Carlstrom Field was reopened to provide primary pilot training for the army and was run by the Riddle Aeronautical Institute. The old derelict World War I buildings, if still standing, were replaced with new and more permanent structures. (Courtesy ADEQ Historical Resources, Inc.)

John Paul Riddle and John G. McKay of the Riddle-McKay Aero College were permitted by the British Air Ministry to establish a facility in Clewiston, near Lake Okeechobee, for the sole purpose of providing primary flight training for RAF personnel. While the airfield in Clewiston was being constructed, the first batch of RAF cadets arrived by train at Arcadia for their training at Carlstrom and Dorr Fields on June 11, 1941. (Courtesy Imperial War Museum.)

Respecting the neutrality of the United States prior to its entry into World War II, the initial recruits from England were dispatched to Toronto, Canada, and brought by train to Florida. As they entered the United States as Canadian citizens, all the cadets were wearing their civilian suits and altered military overcoats. Here cowgirls are shown providing the cadets doughnuts and Florida orange juice. (Courtesy Imperial War Museum.)

Upon their arrival in Arcadia the locals welcomed their English guests. Not everyone understood the need for disguise and the local citizens wondered "why on earth they wanted to come in plain clothes?" (Courtesy Imperial War Museum.)

Cadets received orange juice, tea, coffee, fruits, and other snacks upon their arrival on June 11, 1941. To prepare the Englishmen for the sudden culture shock, the men received instruction booklets on various aspects of American life, geography, and customs. They were ordered not to ask Americans why they had not yet joined in the war or in any manner to be critical of the United States and its neutral status. (Courtesy United States Air Force.)

John Paul Riddle (center) poses with two RAF cadets in front a pile of Florida grapefruits. Riddle had learned flying at Carlstrom Field in the early 1920s. (Courtesy Imperial War Museum.)

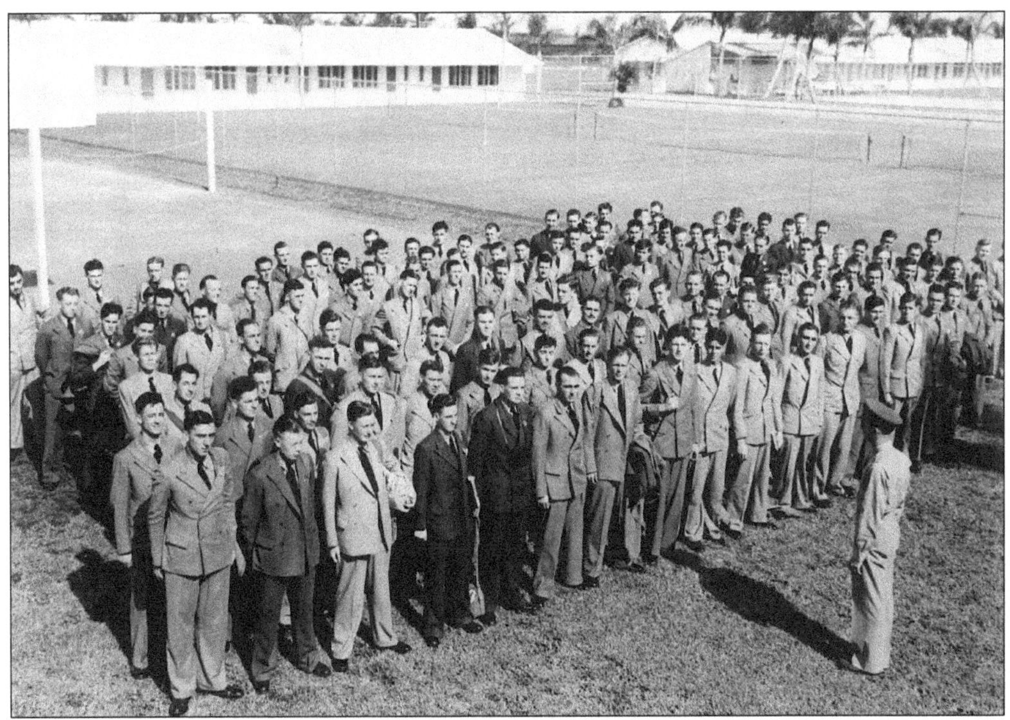

Cadets form up at Carlstrom Field and are introduced to their commanding officer, RAF Wing Commander K.J. Rampling. The first contingent was officially known as British Flying School Squadron 42-A (Course 1). Note the new barracks and tennis courts in the background. (Courtesy Imperial War Museum.)

The cadets gather their belongings and are led to their living quarters. (Courtesy ADEQ Historical Resources, Inc.)

An American cadet, Captain Davis, takes charge of British cadets for their first lineup. (Courtesy Imperial War Museum.)

British cadets are shown here registering at the flight surgeon's office. (Courtesy Imperial War Museum.)

Flight Sergeant Lieutenant Neathery examines the British cadets. (Courtesy Imperial War Museum.)

American cadets of the Riddle Aeronautical Institute are shown presenting the "Union Jack" to British cadets. From left to right in foreground are Lieutenant George Ola (American cadet); Captain Davis (American cadet); RAF Squadron Leader George Burdick; RAF Flight Lieutenant G.W. Nickerson; John Paul Riddle; and Leonard J. Povey (director general of Riddle-McKay Aero College and BFTS #5). At the front of the administrative building a Union Jack would fly at all times with the Stars and Stripes in honor of the British presence at the Arcadia and Clewiston schools. (Courtesy Imperial War Museum.)

British cadets receive their first flying outfits from army supply at the Riddle Aeronautical Institute. The cadets were also issued American military uniforms, such as summer khaki dress and HBT work coveralls. However, the British cadets retained their British military headgear (overseas caps, pith helmets, etc.) and military insignias (rank, wings, specialty designations, etc.) as a distinguishing difference from their American counterparts. (Courtesy Imperial War Museum.)

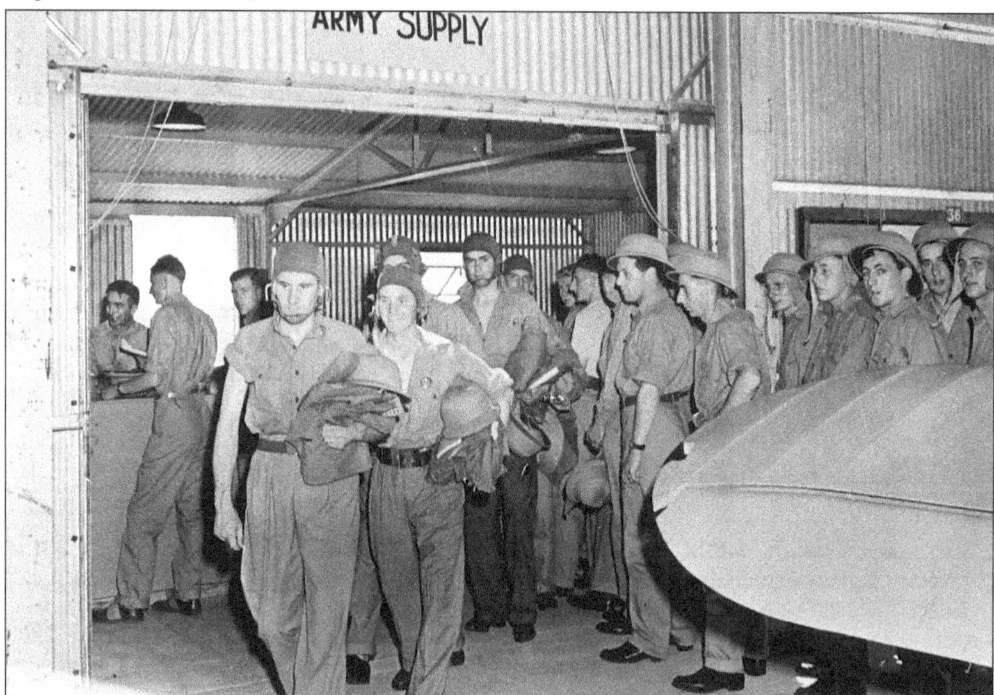

Newly uniformed and equipped British cadets leave the army supply, located in one of the hangars, while their mates await to be outfitted. (Courtesy Imperial War Museum.)

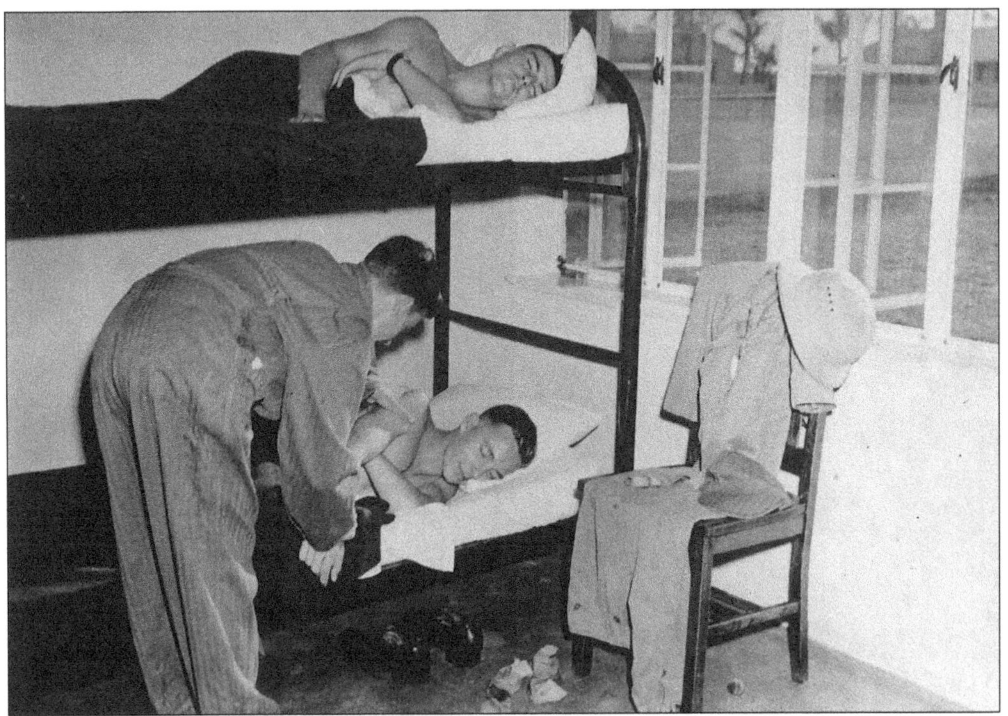
A cadet tries to awaken a fellow cadet for the start of a day's training. (Courtesy Imperial War Museum.)

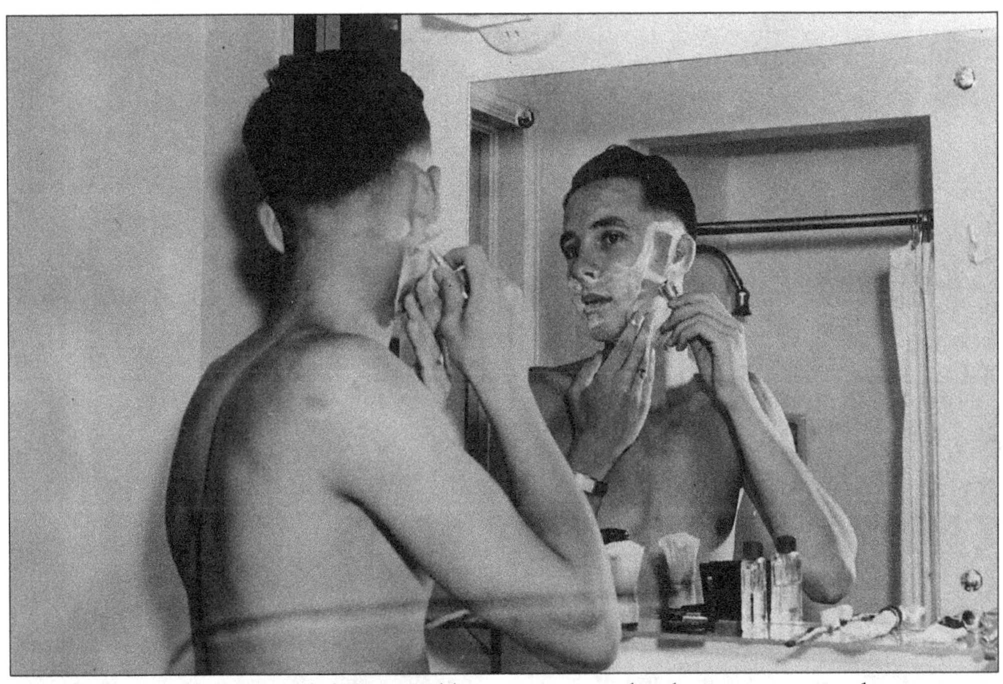
As with every military establishment, soldiers, airmen, and sailors were expected to maintain themselves in a uniform military appearance at all times. Therefore, personal hygiene and grooming were particularly stressed. (Courtesy Imperial War Museum.)

A puzzled trainee ponders over his class notes. (Courtesy Imperial War Museum.)

Cadets are shown here being lectured by a RAI instructor. (Courtesy Imperial War Museum.)

RAF Group Captain D.V. Carnegie congratulates the group flight leader as being the first British cadet to fly off Carlstrom Field as RAI Chief Flight Instructor Jack Hunt looks on. Carnagie worked with Riddle in developing a program for the RAF cadets and providing British government support for the building of the facilities in Clewiston. (Courtesy Imperial War Museum.)

British cadets march toward their aircraft for instruction. (Courtesy ADEQ Historical Resources, Inc.)

An American instructor is seen showing a group of RAF trainees the controls of the aircraft. (Courtesy United States Air Force.)

RAI instructor Dale Delanty is shown surrounded by his students while examining one of their flight goggles. (Courtesy Imperial War Museum.)

A RAF cadet demonstrates his flight equipment to the head officials of BFTS #5. Pictured from right to left are Leonard Povey, John P. Riddle, RAF Group Captain D.V. Carnegie, and RAF Wing Commander K.J. Rampling (in the RAF overseas cap). (Courtesy Imperial War Museum.)

RAF cadets and RAI instructors are shown here on the ramp surrounded by aircraft. (Courtesy United States Air Force.)

British cadets receive instructions for one of their first training flights. (Courtesy United States Air Force.)

Nervous and eager cadets give their Stearman PT-17 the "once over" before their first flight. (Courtesy United States Air Force.)

These five RAF cadets are displaying the different uniforms they arrived at Carlstrom Field with. (Courtesy Imperial War Museum.)

In military order, these RAF cadets are marching off to play a game of baseball. (Courtesy Imperial War Museum.)

A trainee takes a swing at the ball. (Courtesy United States Air Force.)

RAF trainees are shown here during a physical training exercise. The British believed the Florida climate provided ideal conditions in which to make the trainees work. (Courtesy Imperial War Museum.)

Cadets monkey around on the tennis court. Donald Budge served as physical training director for the Riddle Company and was the world's professional tennis champion. He conducted regular tennis clinics. (Courtesy ADEQ Historical Resources, Inc.)

Trainer aircraft are shown here lined up on the airfield at one of the schools, possibly Dorr Field. In the foreground is the duty office where the trainees had to report. (Courtesy Imperial War Museum.)

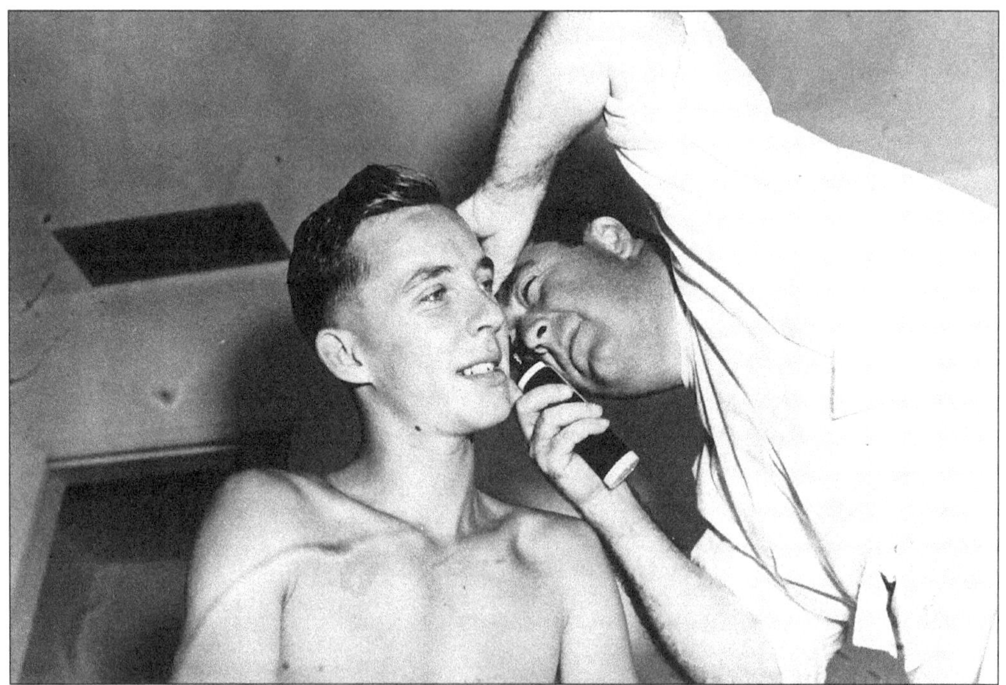

A medical officer checks on the ears of a pupil. Regular medical examinations were required in order to weed out trainees who could not continue or maintain good health. (Courtesy Imperial War Museum.)

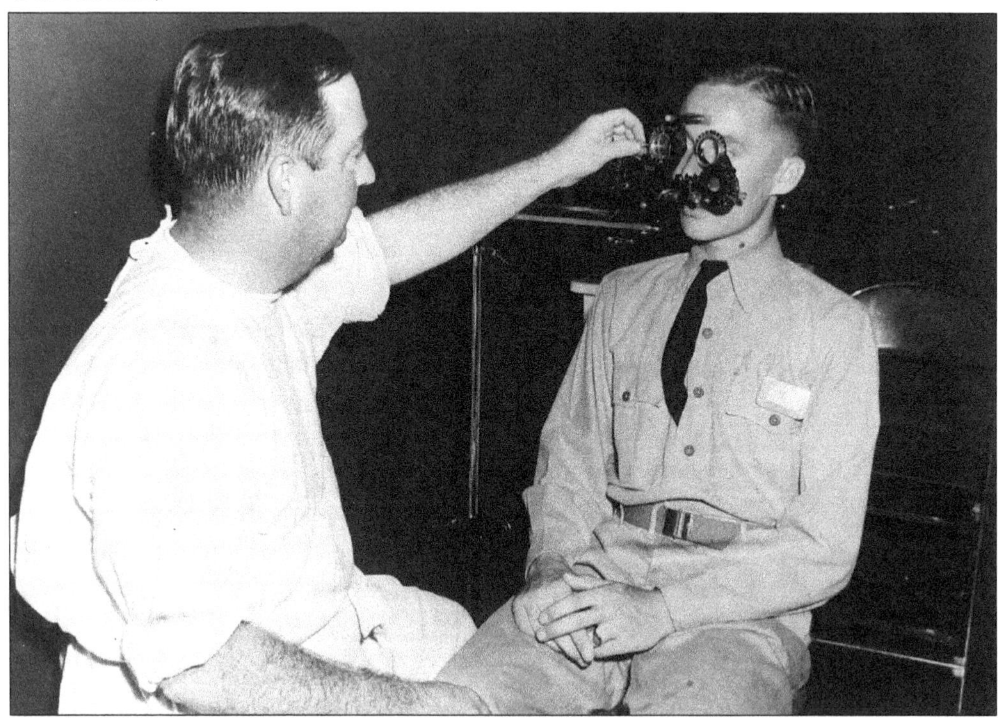

Eye tests on a trainee were quite essential requirements for a pilot. Note the celluloid identity badge worn by the trainee. (Courtesy Imperial War Museum.)

Half of the working hours was occupied by theoretical instruction, while the other half was in practical instruction. (Courtesy Imperial War Museum.)

RAF cadets march toward their trainer aircraft. Note the parachutes. According to a wartime caption, the aircraft in the background "serve the same purpose as the Tiger Moth." (Courtesy ADEQ Historical Resources, Inc.)

The cadets, dressed in darker flight suits, split into sections before taking to the air with their instructors, who are dressed in the lighter suits. (Courtesy Imperial War Museum.)

In the meantime, pupils await the call to a flying lesson at the flying or dispatch office. On the left breast of the flying suit is a tab with the pupils' names. (Courtesy Imperial War Museum.)

Before boarding the aircraft the instructors go over safety inspection and handling of a parachute. (Courtesy Imperial War Museum.)

This was a final inspection by RAF Wing Commander Rampling of the cadets' kits before a flying lesson. (Courtesy Imperial War Museum.)

The cadets were now ready for their flying lessons. (Courtesy Imperial War Museum.)

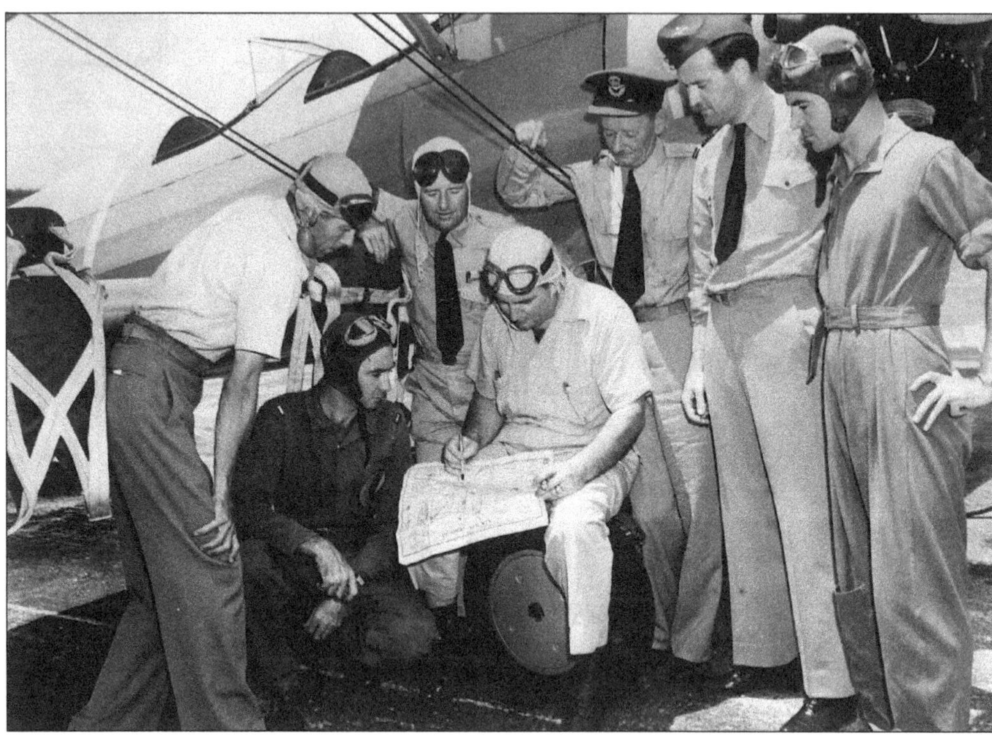

Instructors plot a cross-country flight as RAF Wing Commander Rampling (in the overseas cap) looks on. (Courtesy Imperial War Museum.)

A RAI instructor signs a form allowing aircraft to be taken from the mechanics. (Courtesy Imperial War Museum.)

An instructor shows a trainee the layout of the aircraft controls before a flight begins. (Courtesy Imperial War Museum.)

An instructor, in front of the cadet, radios the tower that they are ready for takeoff. (Courtesy Imperial War Museum.)

Cadets march back toward their barracks. (Courtesy Imperial War Museum.)

The stars and stripes were hoisted at the beginning of each day. The school was awaiting the arrival of a RAF ensign at the time this photograph was taken. Note the administrative building or base headquarters for Carlstrom Field in the background. (Courtesy Imperial War Museum.)

At this particular school they had a modernized version of the dunce's stool of a past era. The offender sits in solitude "on the stool of penitence" reflecting on his error a bad landing. He would remain there until the next offender took his place. (Courtesy Imperial War Museum.)

Arcadia cowboys and cowgirls entertain British cadets with a little advance rodeo show upon their arrival at Carlstrom Field in June 1941. (Courtesy Imperial War Museum.)

Stearman PT-17s weren't the only mounts found by the British cadets. Arcadia cowboys welcomed them with their ponies. (Courtesy Imperial War Museum.)

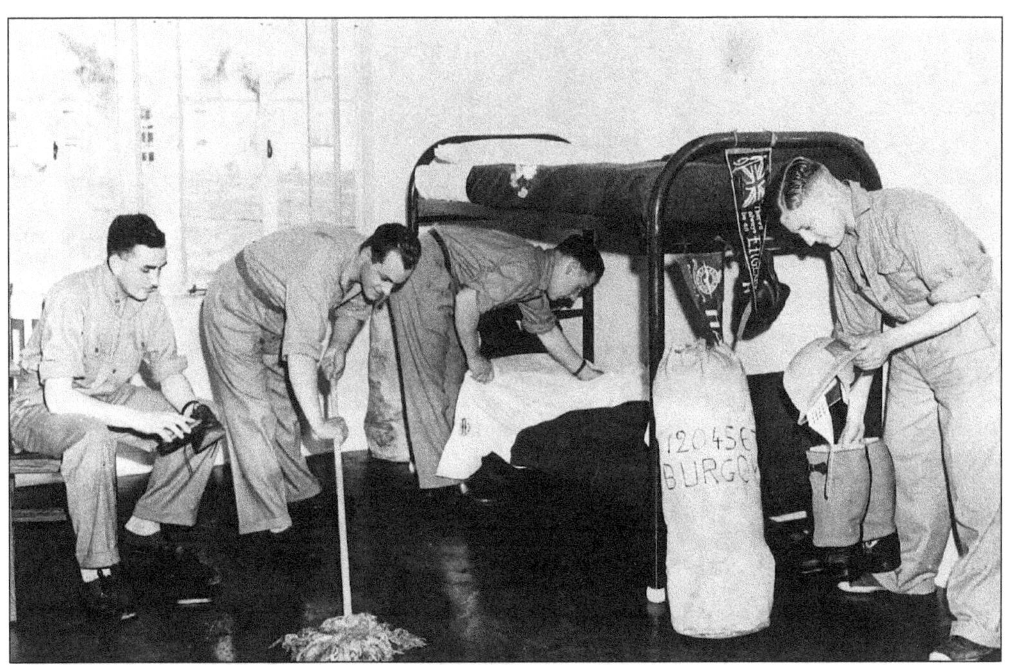

British cadets get their quarters ready for inspection. (Courtesy Imperial War Museum.)

Cadets receive personal attention from their instructor. (Courtesy ADEQ Historical Resources, Inc.)

Attached to the cadet's quarters was a bathing pool. (Courtesy Imperial War Museum.)

There were cinema shows and local girlfriends from Arcadia were permitted to enter the facility. (Courtesy Imperial War Museum.)

Cadets rest in the sunshine outside the mess hall. (Courtesy Imperial War Museum.)

Lunch was served in the mess hall. Note the HBT flight suits being worn by the cadets. A former cadet remembered eating as many eggs as he liked, while back in England he was allowed only one egg a week due to wartime rationing. (Courtesy Imperial War Museum.)

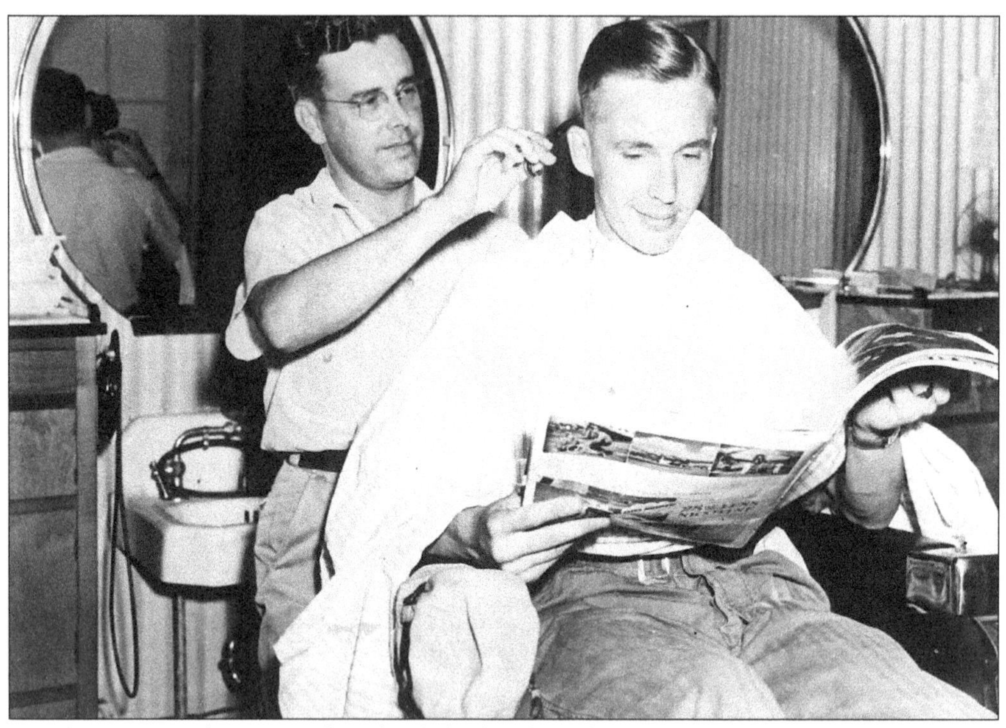

A cadet receives a hair cut at the school's barber shop. (Courtesy Imperial War Museum.)

RAF cadets take a break from the hot Florida sun beside Stearman PT-17 primary trainers provided by the United States Army Air Forces (USAAF). The planes were painted in the bright yellow and blue of the USAAF. (Courtesy Imperial War Museum.)

Soft drinks only were served on the station. The soda fountain was in the recreation room. Note the Coca-Cola and NEHI beverage bottles. (Courtesy Imperial War Museum.)

John Paul Riddle (in white shirt) and RAF Wing Commander Rampling (in visored cap) pose along with the British cadets of Course 1 of British Flying Training School #5 at Carlstrom Field. Note the white flashes on the cadets' overseas caps denoting that they are airmen of the Royal Air Force. (Courtesy Imperial War Museum.)

The USAAF officer commanding the station presents diplomas to the first graduating course. Also present are John Paul Riddle (second from right) and RAF Group Captain Carnegie (second from left), RAF senior member of the air mission at Washington D.C. (Courtesy Imperial War Museum.)

Mr. John P. Riddle presents diplomas to the RAF cadets of Course 1, Class 42-B, at Carlstrom Field on August 16, 1941. The uniforms worn by the cadets are USAAF issue with the exception of their RAF-issued overseas caps. (Courtesy Imperial War Museum.)

Mr. Riddle personally congratulates a RAF cadet on August 16, 1941. With pressure by the USAAF for more needed space at Carlstrom and Dorr Fields, the British began their move to the at-the-time-unfinished Riddle Field in Clewiston. On September 25, 1941, 89 cadets from Arcadia arrived at the Clewiston site. However, some RAF cadets continued to train at Carlstrom Field until late April 1942, when the Clewiston facility was completed. (Courtesy Imperial War Museum.)

Three

British Flying Training School #5: Riddle Field, Clewiston

Construction of the Clewiston site began a month after the arrival of the RAF cadets at Arcadia. While looking for suitable sites for a permanent RAF school, John Riddle and RAF Group Captain Carnegie flew near Clewiston. After Carnegie expressed concern that a site had not been picked yet, Riddle turned his aircraft engine off and exclaimed that where the plane lands would be the site of the school. He landed the plane smoothly in an area 7 miles near Clewiston. (Courtesy Clewiston Museum.)

This is another aerial view of the BFTS #5 facility in Clewiston. There were legal problems in the acquisition of the land for the school. The 140 state-owned acres weren't the problem, it was the various private properties that Riddle needed to complete his facility. The State of Florida permitted Riddle to take title of the disputed properties by eminent domain and agreed to tackle the issue of ownership in the next meeting of the Florida Legislature in September 1941. Therefore, construction began on the site on July 17, 1941, before legal acquisition of the land. (Courtesy Clewiston Museum.)

Frank Wheeler of the Wheeler Construction Company in Miami was awarded the contract for British Flying Training School #5 at Clewiston. Wheeler was also responsible for the construction for many of the new buildings of the Riddle Aero. Institute at Arcadia. (Courtesy Clewiston Museum.)

Upon the cadet's arrival at Riddle Field on September 25, 1941, only two barracks and a mess hall had been completed. The other buildings were still under construction. (Courtesy Clewiston Museum.)

Mixed in with the ranks of RAF cadets were a number of Americans who volunteered for service in Britain's fight against Hitler's blitzkrieging Luftwaffe. These men gained valuable experience in the early stages of the war. Upon the American entry into the war after Pearl Harbor, many of these "Yanks" transferred back to the United States Army Air Corps to train fighter and bomber pilots and command combat squadrons. (ADEQ Historical Resources, Inc.)

The station headquarters is shown here upon its completion in the fall of 1941. (ADEQ Historical Resources, Inc.)

This 1941 photograph shows the radio tower and flight executive offices at Riddle Field, home of British Flying Training School #5. (ADEQ Historical Resources, Inc.)

By December 20, 1941, the swimming pool was completed and placed in operation. Note the hangar in the background. (Courtesy Clewiston Museum.)

This aerial view shows Riddle Field as it appeared toward the end of 1941. The facility began receiving newer and more powerful aircraft trainers—the BT-13 and the AT-6. (Courtesy Clewiston Museum.)

"The end of a long journey and the start of another." Newly graduated cadets with their RAF wings sewn to their tunics are shown here leaving Clewiston. Note that they are wearing their RAF uniforms; they were no longer required to wear civilian attire in public after America's entry into war following the attack on Pearl Harbor on December 7, 1941. (ADEQ Historical Resources, Inc.)

This detachment of RAF cadets was photographed at the train station of Clewiston. There was a steady stream of British personnel going to and leaving from Riddle Field throughout the war. (ADEQ Historical Resources, Inc.)

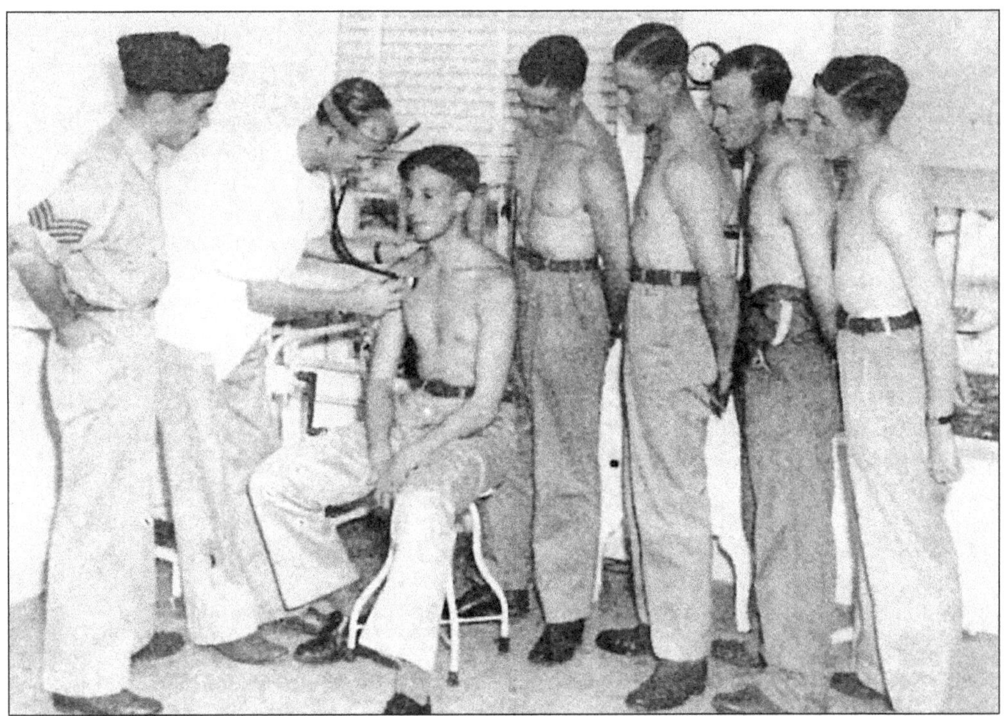

RAF Sergeant J. Henley (far left) overlooks the medical examination conducted by Dr. T. Gowin of new arrivals to Riddle Field. Sergeant Henley was part of the permanent RAF staff for BFTS #5 and served as clerk accounts. (ADEQ Historical Resources, Inc.)

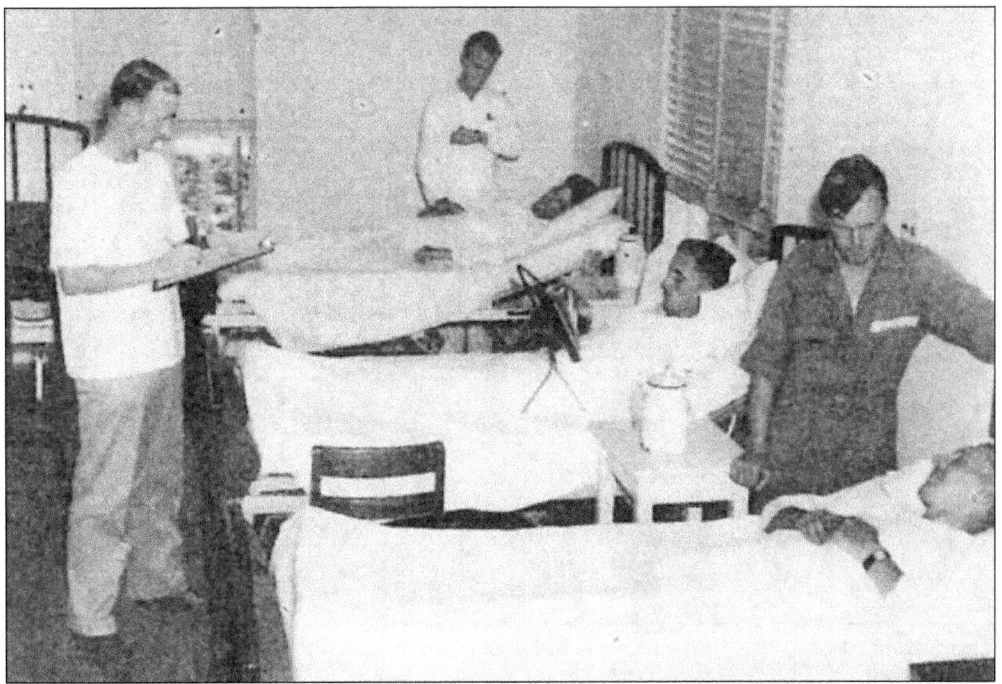

For those cadets who fell ill or were injured in accidents, a modern hospital and ward were constructed at the school. (ADEQ Historical Resources, Inc.)

Mr. Fred E. Hunziker was the Officer Commanding of Number Two Squadron. Cadets and instructors were split into two training squadrons. Number One Squadron consisted of Basic (Blue) and Advance (Red) Flights, while Number Two Squadron consisted of Primary (Yellow and Green) Flights. (ADEQ Historical Resources, Inc.)

The Advanced (Red) Flight instructors of Number One Squadron pose for a photograph. They are, from left to right, as follows: (front row) K. Lang Horne, K. Woodward, N.C. Ellis, C.W. Miller, R. Morders, L. Place, and, C.W. Bing; (back row) H.J. Middleton, J.F. Reahard, A.E. McCravy, R. Westmoreland, T. Teate, and W.R. King. (ADEQ Historical Resources, Inc.)

A skeet range was also provided for the training of cadets while attending BFTS #5. (ADEQ Historical Resources, Inc.)

Fifty cadets arrived at Riddle Field on December 4, 1941, as Course 5. They received their training and returned to England via Moncton, Canada, by mid-June of 1942. Note the row of North American AT-6 Advanced Trainers in the background. (Courtesy Clewiston Museum.)

Cadets from the Basic Flight Line (Number One Squadron) receiving last minute instructions from their instructor before taking a night flight. (ADEQ Historical Resources, Inc.)

An instructor wishes his student good luck as he boards an AT-6. Many of the deaths that occurred at the school were from night flying. (ADEQ Historical Resources, Inc.)

A group of RAF trainees stand in formation on the ramp with AT-6 Trainers in the background. Note the white flash in the overseas caps denoting aircrews and the USAAF-issue khaki uniforms being worn by the British cadets. (ADEQ Historical Resources, Inc.)

Air Marshall G. Garrod visited Riddle Field during one of the graduations held by the school, 1941–42. Pictured are, from left to right, Air Commodore D.V. Carnegie, RAF; Captain Price, USAAF; Major Carl Feldman, USAAF; General Clarence Tinker, USAAF (Commanding Officer of MacDill Army Air Base in Tampa); Air Marshall Garrod, RAF; General George E. Stratemeyer, USAAF; Wing Commander W. Oulton, RAF; Mr. G. Willis Tyson (General Manager of Riddle-McKay Aero College, killed after landing at Tallhassee on August 18, 1943); Squadron Leader George Burdick, RAF; Mr. Leonard J. Povey (Director General of Riddle-McKay Aero College); Wing Commander K.J. Rampling, RAF; Mr. John Paul Riddle; and Group Commander Douglas Hamilton, RAF. (ADEQ Historical Resources, Inc.)

Air Commodore D.V. Carnegie inspects a cadet's quarters. (Courtesy Clewiston Museum.)

Accidents occurred because the school was forced to pump out a large number of pilots in a wartime atmosphere. Seen here are two PT-17s, most probably damaged while either taking off or landing. Both occupants escaped injuries from this accident. (Courtesy Peter Brannan)

This PT-17 ended up on its back after a crash landing. (Courtesy Clewiston Museum.)

Note the school buildings in the background of this photograph of a crashed AT-6 at Riddle Field. Many more fatalities occurred in these sophisticated trainers than in the Stearman PT-17 Primary Trainers. (Courtesy Clewiston Museum.)

RAF cadets pay their final respects to recently fallen comrades in Arcadia's Oak Ridge Cemetery. In all, 23 cadets were buried at this cemetery from 1941 to 1945. Not all deaths were trainees; PT-17 Instructors A.R. Thompson and Fred G. Howe were killed while training cadets. (Courtesy Clewiston Museum.)

"Ah Sure Likes Ta Fly." This image of an African American in a stripped AT-6 and its caption were found in an anniversary booklet of the BFTS's first year in operation. It is not known if the British cadets found this to be humorous; one is reminded that Florida was still a part of the Old South where Jim Crow Laws and segregation were a fact of life. Many African Americans fought against racism in their own ways to earn respect—such as the Tuskegee Airmen. (Courtesy ADEQ Historical Resources, Inc.)

Hugh Williams (center) trained as a cadet in the early phases of Riddle Field when the first courses (2 and 3) were transferred there from Carlstrom Field in September 1941. (Courtesy Hugh Williams.)

Upon graduation from BFTS #5, Hugh Williams received his RAF wings and his sergeant chevrons. He returned to Great Britain and served honorably throughout World War II. (Courtesy Hugh Williams.)

Not all cadets attending BFTS #5 were RAF. Lieutenant John W. Cook and 16 other USAAF cadets attended the school with Course 14 from March 18, 1943, to October 1, 1943. Note the wings of both the Royal Air Force and the United States Army Air Force on his uniform. (Courtesy John W. Cook.)

Cadets march toward one of the lecture rooms. (Courtesy Clewiston Museum.)

These photographs show the interior of the school's library. Note the school's honor roll plaques near the entrance in the image below. (Courtesy ADEQ Historical Resources, Inc.)

This is the interior of the Link Trainer Building, where cadets went for a "spin" in the link. (Courtesy ADEQ Historical Resources, Inc.)

RAF Wing Commander Greaves shoots up field on July 4, 1943. (Courtesy John W. Cook.)

BFTS Instructor Neil Mangold and RAF Lance Air Corporal Garland of Rhodesia stand in front of an AT-6. Note the instructor is wearing RAF-style cap insignia and wings, with the letters "BFTS" instead of the royal crown on them. (Courtesy John W. Cook.)

This sign stood at the entrance of the school. (Courtesy John W. Cook.)

Cadets form up for parade in front of Riddle Field's hangars. (Courtesy ADEQ Historical Resources, Inc.)

Course 6 arrived at Riddle Field for training on January 25, 1942. This group photo was taken on August 5 of that year, prior to their transfer to Moncton, Canada. Among those pictured here are RAF Flight Lieutenant G.W. Nickerson, BFTS administrative officer (seated fourth from left); RAF Wing Commander Rampling, BFTS commanding officer (seated fifth from left); Leonard Povey, director general (seated fourth from right); and RAF Flying Officer William Rienhart, BFTS navigation officer (seated third from right). (Courtesy Clewiston Museum.)

RAF cadets of Course 10 trained at Riddle Field from August 1942 to February 1943. (Courtesy Clewiston Museum.)

This photograph was simply captioned "Corporal Helliwell & Marie, Course 10 (1942–43)." "Marie" was Mary Edna Parker, who worked as a secretary at Riddle Field. (Courtesy Clewiston Museum.)

Cadets perform a variety show for their comrades. (Courtesy ADEQ Historical resources, Inc.)

Mr. and Mrs. Nesmith welcomed many homesick RAF cadets to their Clewiston home for social gatherings. (Courtesy Peter Brannan.)

The Nesmith's home was fondly called the "Furlough House" by the RAF cadets. This photograph, dated September 9, 1945, shows cadets from Course 24, 25, and 26 of British Flying Training School #5 on the lawn of the Nesmith's Clewiston home. (Courtesy Clewiston Museum.)

This informal photograph of BFTS flight instructors was taken at Riddle Field. Many of these men formed the Instructor's Club. Located at a house at 325 East Delmonte in Clewiston, the club was used for after-hours recreation. (Courtesy Eric Carlson.)

A and B Flights of Course 12 were trained at BFTS #5 from November 12, 1942, to May 25, 1943. Note the control tower in the background and the flying of both the "Stars and Stripes" and the "Union Jack." (Courtesy Clewiston Museum.)

This is a wartime view of the control tower. (Courtesy ADEQ Historical Resources, Inc.)

The flight line recorder and flight commander are shown here. Note the row of Stearman trainers in the background. (Courtesy Eric Carlson.)

Cadets and instructors approach their aircraft for advanced flight training. (Courtesy ADEQ Historical Resources, Inc.)

This AT-6 Trainer was photographed while airborne. (Courtesy ADEQ Historical Resources, Inc.)

Flying Officer William Rienhart (left), Mr. Fred Hunziker (center, in dark shirt), and Wing Commander George Greaves go over the day's training activities in 1943. W/C Greaves (CO from January 27, 1943, to November 10, 1943) was one of five RAF officers who commanded BFTS #5 from 1941 to 1945. (Courtesy John W. Cook.)

As a moral booster the school would bring about a day's worth of competitive sports every three months. Seen here are Wing Commander K.J. Rampling and Squadron Leader George Burdick after a three-legged race on Sports Day, April 4, 1942. (Courtesy ADEQ Historical Resources, Inc.)

This potato sack race took place on one of the Sports Days. (Courtesy ADEQ Historical Resources, Inc.)

This friendly game of tug-o-war was photographed on April 4, 1942. (Courtesy ADEQ Historical Resources, Inc.)

A track meet was held at Riddle Field in May 1943. (Courtesy John W. Cook.)

A formation of AT-6 Advanced Trainers is shown here from a cockpit. (Courtesy John W. Cook.)

"Duffy and Queeny" pose for the camera. Queenie became the school's official mascot and appeared numerous times in the *Embry-Riddle Fly Paper*, the school's newspaper. Local lore has it that Queenie, a stray mixed breed dog, would regularly board the bus in Clewiston to spend the day receiving attention from the cadets at the school and then return home on the bus at the end of the day. It was said she had a fondness for English leather. After the war one of the secretaries from the school took Queenie home with her and the lucky dog lived out a happy life. (Courtesy ADEQ Historical Resources, Inc.)

The cantina was where refreshments and recreation awaited cadets after a hard day's training. (Courtesy ADEQ Historical Resources, Inc.)

An unidentified group of RAF cadets pose in front of an AT-6 with the control tower in the background. One cadet recounted "We came over from England, which was total blackout, which was cold, which was out of food, and we came into sunshine. The whole place was lit up like a beacon." (Courtesy ADEQ Historical Resources, Inc.)

Wing Commander Greaves, Flight Lieutenant Nickerson, and G. Willis Tyson (seated with sunglasses and visored cap) were photographed at a school event. Nickerson died in July 1943, while General Manager Tyson was killed when the wing of a P-47 clipped his plane while landing at Dale Mabry Field in Tallahassee on August 18, 1943. (Courtesy John W. Cook.)

A B-25 sits on the ramp at Riddle Field. With USAAF bases nearby, planes from these facilities would occasionally land at the field for one reason or another. This also provided hands-on familiarity with these aircraft by the RAF and USAAF trainees of BFTS #5. (Courtesy John W. Cook.)

A Lockheed A-29 Hudson Bomber Trainer is in the foreground of this photograph. Note the hangars and control tower in the distance. In 1942, with the U.S. facing a serious U-boat threat along the East Coast, a number of Hudsons were delivered to USAAF squadrons. (Courtesy John W. Cook.)

American and British cadets, as differentiated by their headgear, march past guests at a school event at the field. (Courtesy Clewiston Museum.)

The leading cadets were identified by armbands denoting the appointed rank of flight or squadron leaders, as can be seen with careful scrutiny in this parade of cadets. (Courtesy Clewiston Museum.)

An inspection of the cadets, instructors, aircraft, and the school took place annually. Note the various training aircraft used by the school. (Courtesy ADEQ Historical Resources, Inc.)

Instructors stand in formation during an inspection. (Courtesy ADEQ Historical Resources, Inc.)

This was the swimming pool of BFTS #5. (Courtesy John W. Cook.)

Clewiston residents and cadets are shown here at an indoor function in one of the school's buildings. The people in Clewiston were very hospitable to their English guests throughout the war years. (Courtesy ADEQ Historical Resources, Inc.)

Cadets in their RAF uniforms march past dignitaries during a graduation ceremony. (Courtesy Clewiston Museum.)

Wing Commander Rampling gives cadets a last minute inspection before the 1942 graduation ceremony. (Courtesy Clewiston Museum.)

RAF Air Marshall D.S.C. Evill presents wings to a RAF cadet on Graduation Day. Note the box of sergeant chevrons on the table to be awarded during the ceremony. (Courtesy Clewiston Museum.)

Mr. Riddle congratulates a RAF cadet upon receiving his wings. (Courtesy Clewiston Museum.)

An American cadet is congratulated by John Paul Riddle upon receiving his wings from British Flying Training School #5. Note the distinctive cap insignia of the BFTS worn by Mr. Povey on the far left as compared to that worn by the RAF officer on the far right. (Courtesy Clewiston Museum.)

Air Marshall Evill addresses the cadets during graduation. (Courtesy Clewiston Museum.)

RAF cadets Larry Beale and Ginger Morris of Course 14 in 1943. (Courtesy John W. Cook.)

Cadets from Course 14 bicycle while on leave to West Palm Beach in August 1943. They have been identified as Maurice Venn, Bonsey, Fred Cor, Cartwright, Comtrill, Murdock, and Harry Randall. (Courtesy John W. Cook.)

An unidentified cadet of Course 14 poses on a trainer at Riddle Field. (Courtesy John W. Cook.)

RAF cadets form up for the graduation of Course 13, July 29, 1943. (Courtesy John W. Cook.)

Cadets from Course 13 are shown here being presented their wings. (Courtesy John W. Cox.)

Cadets march off with their wings and certificates of completing their flight training. (Courtesy John W. Cook.)

John Bevan of the RAF is shown here in August 1943. (Courtesy John W. Cook.)

John Bevan, "Swanny," George Goodinson, and Grimer of Course 13 were photographed in August 1943. (Courtesy John W. Cook.)

Recently graduated cadets of Course 14 await for their train trip back to Canada, and the war, at the Clewiston Train Station in October 1943.

RAF and USAAF cadets of Course 15 arrived to the school on May 26, 1943, and graduated from BFTS #5 on December 3, 1943. (Courtesy Clewiston Museum.)

Course 18 trained at BFTS #5 from December 17, 1943, to June 17, 1944. (Courtesy Clewiston Museum.)

Unidentified RAF and USAAF cadets smile after receiving their wings. Throughout the years when BFTS #5 was in operation there were five RAF commanding officers: W/C K.J. Rampling (July 1941–August 1942); W/C T.C. Prickett (August 1942–January 1943); W/C Greaves (January 1943–November 1943); W/C de Gruyther (November 1943–April 1944); W/C Lindsay (April 1944–September 1945). (Courtesy Clewiston Museum.)

The last class to attend BFTS #5 was Course 26, which arrived on June 19, 1945. Course 24, however, was the last to officially graduate; they did so on August 25, 1945. (Courtesy Clewiston Museum.)

During its four years of operation, 1,879 cadets began training at Arcadia and Clewiston, and 1,452 received their wings. British Flying Training School #5 was closed on September 10, 1945. (Courtesy Clewiston Museum.)

"Hip, Hip . . ." (Courtesy Imperial War Museum.)

"Hoorah!" This work is dedicated to the memory of the 23 RAF cadets buried in Arcadia with their instructor, John Paul Riddle. (Courtesy Imperial War Museum.)

Four

Memories and Ghosts

At the Clewiston train station, a recently graduated cadet looks back for the last time at what was home for six months before boarding his train to an uncertain future. (Courtesy John W. Cook.)

The former hangars of the Lodwick School of Aeronautics still stand in Lakeland. (Photographed by the Author.)

The hangars and the ramp are now maintained by the City of Lakeland Parks and Recreation Department for use as exhibitions or to house club events. (Photographed by the Author.)

The hangars are the only structures left of the old aviation school. (Photographed by the Author.)

The aviation school's runways are now used as roads leading into the complex. (Photographed by the Author.)

Around 1993 the old mess hall of Lodwick Field was torn down to make way for the new general offices of the Detroit Tigers. The baseball team made Lodwick Field its winter home and shares the site with the city of Lakeland. (Photographed by the Author.)

One of the only standing structures of the Lodwick Military Aviation Academy is this hangar near Avon Park. (Photographed by the Author.)

Today the hangar is home to a boat manufacturing company. (Photographed by the Author.)

After the war the former hotel and military school in Avon Park became the Walker Memorial Sanitarium and Hospital. (Photographed by the Author.)

The old Lodwick Military Aviation Academy, no longer in use, is shown here in 1997, in a view taken looking across Lake Lillian from the school's abandoned tennis court. The athletic fields for the school were located across the lake, now overgrown with homes. (Photographed by the Author.)

The tennis court, as well as the abandoned hospital, are the only remnants of the Lodwick Military Aviation Academy. (Photographed by the Author.)

Dorr Field, near Arcadia, closed in November 1945. The field's buildings were used as a Florida State Hospital and later became the site for a correctional facility. (Courtesy ADEQ Historical Resources, Inc.)

This is a post-war aerial view of Carlstrom Field. Both Dorr and Carlstrom Fields, where over 7,500 cadets trained, were closed in November 1945. Carlstrom Field is now home to the G. Pierce Wood Memorial Hospital, a state hospital for mental patients. (Courtesy ADEQ Historical Resources, Inc.)

Carlstrom Field's former headquarters still serve as an administrative building for the hospital complex. This photograph was taken in November 1994. (Photographed by the Author.)

The mess hall also continues to serve its original purpose. (Photographed by the Author.)

The two remaining wartime hangars and the water tower at Carlstrom Field are shown here. (Photographed by the Author.)

This hangar is in an excellent state of preservation. Many of the buildings that make up the hospital complex are still used; the hanger shown here now serves as a maintenance shop. (Photographed by the Author.)

Many of the barracks and class buildings are still standing. Note the hangars in the background of this November 1994 photograph. (Courtesy ADEQ Historical Resources, Inc.)

The Union Jack flies over the British plot in Arcadia's Oak Ridge Cemetery 24 hours a day, 365 days a year. (Photographed by the Author.)

The RAF cadets lie side by side in eternal rest. J.P. Riddle, their wartime instructor, joined them in 1989. (Photographed by the Author.)

The headstones of the cadets bear the RAF seal. Only Riddle's headstone displays the World War II-style U.S. Army Air cadet insignia. (Photographed by the Author.)

Every day the sun warms the cadets' headstones in the morning and sets behind them in the evening. (Photographed by the Author.)

In 1947 the former Riddle Field reopened as Airglades State Airport. The field's old control tower, now reduced, became a derelict by the late 1960s. (Courtesy ADEQ Historical Resources, Inc.)

An abandoned building at Riddle Field is shown here in the late 1960s. (Courtesy ADEQ Historical Resources, Inc.)

By the 1970s most, if not all, of the buildings were razed. The old cantina had deteriorated significantly by the time this photograph was taken. (Courtesy ADEQ Historical Resources, Inc.)

Today, the only standing structure of British Flying Training School #5 is this maintenance hangar, shown here in October 1997. (Photographed by the Author.)

This panoramic view of the entrance to Riddle Field was taken in October 1997. Virtually nothing remains of the school today, with the exception of the maintenance hangar. (Photographed by the Author.)

A reunion of former British cadets, wearing their RAF unit ties, took place at the Clewiston Inn in 1986. Many of the veterans have formed a group known as the No. 5 British Flying Training School Association. Those shown here, listed here from left to right with their course numbers, are as follows: (front row) P.A. Brannan (#25); P.F. Wilson (#3); A. Hall (#19); S.J. Slape (#6); and M.L. Hammond (#23); (middle row) H.R. Eustace (#22); R. Kerry (#5); G. Beardmore (#24); T.K. Clanzy (#9); H. Leeks (#5); H.T. Wilkin (#12); R.M. Cox (#22); R. Dawson (#22); and G. Newsham (#24); (back row) H. Guile (#15); R.B. Peters (#26); R.W. Warburton (#16); John Paul Riddle; R.J. Searle (#18); C.E.P. Jackson (#20); Sir J. Heywood (#17); I. Loch (#7); and H. Button (#8). (Courtesy Clewiston Museum.)

This is the former BFTS #5 instructors' clubhouse on 325 East Del Monte Avenue in Clewiston. (Photographed by the Author.)

Amongst the many artifacts in the Clewiston Museum is this instructor's tunic. (Photographed by the Author.)

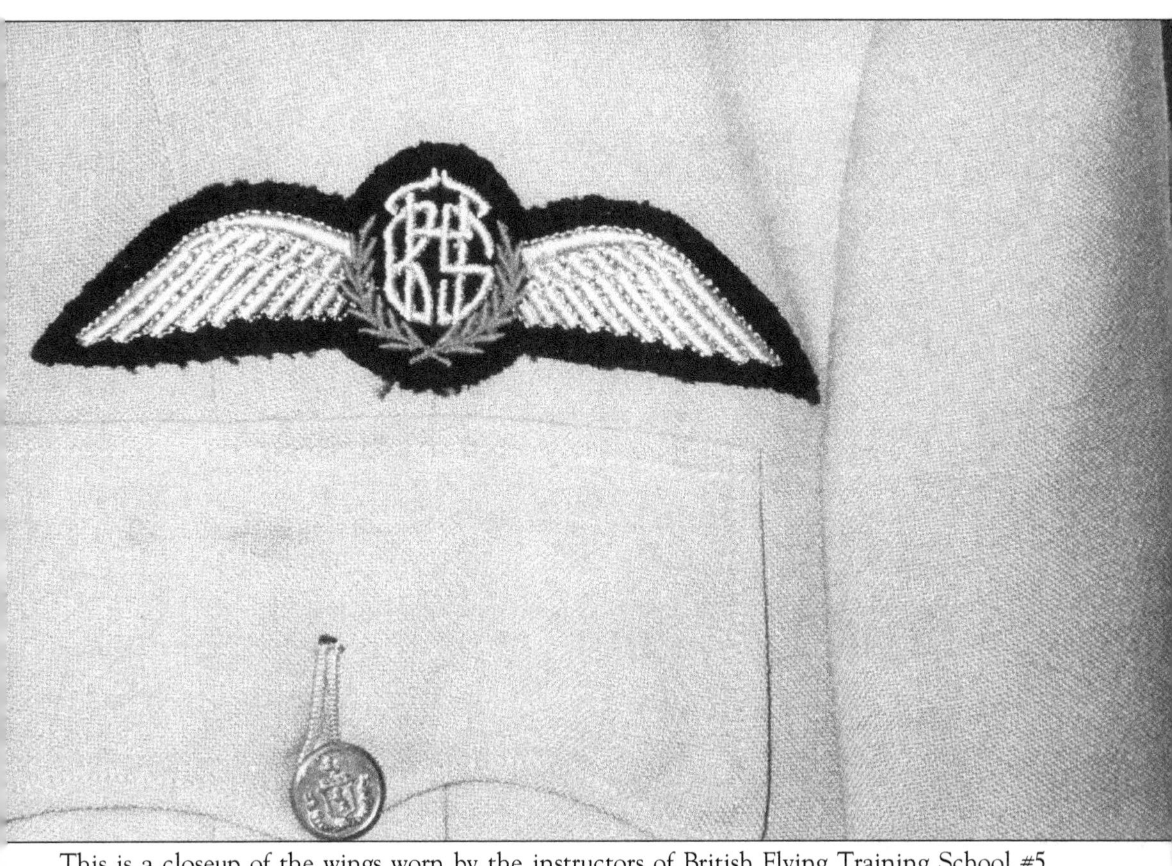

This is a closeup of the wings worn by the instructors of British Flying Training School #5. (Photographed by the Author.)

The City of Clewiston and former cadets placed a memorial in Civic Center Park on Sugarland Highway in honor of the RAF cadets and the school they attended during World War II. (Photographed by the Author.)

www.ingramcontent.com/pod-product-compliance
Lightning Source LLC
LaVergne TN
LVHW081554100826
845153LV00004B/378

9781531645335